A Call To Worship

Worship Aids

Lectionary Year B

Frank Ramirez

CSS Publishing Company, Inc., Lima, Ohio

A CALL TO WORSHIP

Copyright © 2002 by
CSS Publishing Company, Inc.
Lima, Ohio

Library of Congress Cataloging-in-Publication Data

Ramirez, Frank, 1954-
  A call to worship : worship aids, lectionary year B / Frank Ramirez.
    p. cm.
  ISBN 0-7880-1898-1 (pbk. : alk. paper)
  1. Church of the Brethren—Liturgy—Texts. 2. Common lectionary (1992). Year B. I. Title.
  BX7825 .R36 2002
  264'.13—dc21   2002004186

For more information about CSS Publishing Company resources, visit our website at www.csspub.com or e-mail us at custserv@csspub.com or call (800) 241-4056.

ISBN 0-7880-1898-1
PRINTED IN U.S.A.

Dedicated to my brother Michael

We missed being twins by a mere eleven months, but had pretty much everything else in common during our otherwise shared childhood, including, ultimately, a love for the Lord.

Table Of Contents

Introduction

These Calls to Worship, Litanies, Morning Prayers, Offering Prayers, and Children's Benedictions were largely written during the Liturgical Year 1999-2000, and reflect the way the Sundays fell during that repetition of the Year B cycle. I have relied upon the Revised Common Lectionary, and made use of Old Testament texts, especially the Psalms, when they would suit, although these resources bear witness to the New Testament readings as well.

The Children's Benedictions may require some explanation. During the final hymn those children who wish may come forward to pronounce this benedictory sentence. Those who can read are handed a sheet with the words. Those who are too young to read are told the sentence. They rehearse the sentence quietly during the hymn, and then recite it in unison to close the service.

A final word of explanation. Most of the resources either came from my pen, or were translated by me, with the exception of three famous texts (St. Richard of Chichester's "Day by Day," "We Plow The Fields and Scatter" by Matthias Claudius, and "Let All Mortal Flesh Keep Silence" from the *Liturgy of St. James of Jerusalem*, fifth c.; translated by Gerard Moultrie, *Lyra Eucharistica,* second edition, 1864).

There is one modern hymn, however, included as a resource, free of charge. It is "Move In Our Midst" by Ken Morse.

In my denomination the late Ken Morse was famous as a poet, hymn writer, editor, and author. He was most renowned for his hymn "Move In Our Midst." This hymn is one of the most beloved of the Brethren. The tune was written by Perry Lee Huffaker, and appeared in the 1951 *The Brethren Hymnal*, as well as the 1992 *Hymnal: A Worship Book*. Morse wrote the first two stanzas while at Camp Harmony in western Pennsylvania. The final two stanzas were commissioned specifically for the 1951 hymnal. According to the story, the tune itself was composed by Huffaker while he rode in a car with Morse to a church engagement.

Through an administrative oversight the copyright for this hymn, along with many other Brethren resources, was not renewed, and it is therefore in the public domain. Ken Morse always encouraged me in my writing, and it is as a tribute to him that I am including it in this resource book.

Frank Ramirez
March, 2001

First Sunday Of Advent

Advent Wreath
We come with open minds.
We light this first candle as we recall the past
and all that God has done for us.
We come with open hearts
as we look to the future and God's promises yet to be fulfilled.
In our troubled world we pray
that this candle will become the light of hope for ourselves and all
whom we serve.

Call To Worship (based on Isaiah 64)

One:	O that you would tear open the heavens and come down, so that the mountains would quake at your presence —
All:	as when fire kindles brushwood and the fire causes water to boil — to make your name known to your adversaries, so that the nations might tremble at your presence!
Men:	When you did awesome deeds that we did not expect, you came down; the mountains quaked at your presence.
Women:	From ages past no one has heard, no ear has perceived, no eye has seen any God besides you, who works for those who wait for him.
Young:	You meet those who gladly do right, those who remember you in your ways. But you were angry, and we sinned; because you hid yourself we transgressed.
Old:	We have all become like one who is unclean, and all our righteous deeds are like a filthy cloth. We all fade like a leaf, and our iniquities, like the wind, take us away.
One:	There is no one who calls on your name, or attempts to take hold of you; for you have hidden your face from us, and have delivered us into the hand of our iniquity.
All:	Yet, O LORD, you are our Father; we are the clay, and you are our potter; we are all the work of your hand.

Unison Prayer
Lord, again we come to the Advent season. We've been here before. We've never walked upon this ground. We've sung these songs before. We've never sung them like this. The thoughts of our favorite foods and customs fill us with joy. The dread of loneliness and sorrow fills us with dread. We celebrate the coming of the Christ Child in Bethlehem two thousand years ago, but look forward as well to the return of Jesus at the end of time. Help us to look forward and backward during this season. We anticipate again the coming of the Christ Child in Bethlehem, but also look forward to the return of Jesus at the end of time. Give meaning and shape to our gathering. Bless us in this moment, and throughout this season. Amen.

Morning Prayer
This day, Gracious God, we come to you, with our joys and concerns, our celebrations and our sorrows. All the experiences of our lives we lay upon the altar, with the prayer that as you hear them, you will answer our prayers in your wisdom according to your will. In Jesus' name we pray. Amen.

Offering Message
Lord, at this time we bring to you the gifts of our hands and hearts, the fruit of our labor, the emblem of what we cherish, both for what it would have bought for us, and also for what it will do for you. Magnify these gifts beyond their physical measure. Perform great miracles through our halting generosity. Amen.

Children's Benediction
Keep awake! Get ready for the celebration!

Second Sunday Of Advent

Advent Wreath
We come with many fears and anxieties.
We light this second candle to remind us of your faithfulness.
Get ready, one and all.
In the impatient world in which we live,
may these candles light and prepare the way into your loving arms.

Call To Worship

One:	The Evangelist Mark reminded us of the words of the prophets:
All:	"See, I am sending my messenger ahead of you, who will prepare your way;
Men:	"the voice of one crying out in the wilderness:
Women:	" 'Prepare the way of the Lord, make his paths straight.' "
One:	We have a past as individuals.
All:	We have a past as Christians.
Front:	Time to get ready.
Back:	Get ready for the Lord!
All:	Lord, we seek your comfort promised to your people.
One:	We seek your new life.

Morning Prayer (based on Isaiah 40)
Comfort your people, as you promised the prophet Isaiah. Speak tenderly to us, because sometimes we feel as if we have received double for all our sins. Reveal your glory, that all people shall see it together. We pledge to climb your high mountain, to be your heralds, to say to one and all, "Here is your God!" You come with might, Lord God. You are our shepherd. Gather us in your arms as we gather ourselves to worship you and praise your name. Lead us. Guide us. Uphold us. Inspire us. Amen.

Morning Prayer
Heavenly Father, there are times when we get so tired, and it seems that nothing matters much. We recall the words of your prophet,

that the grass withers and the flower fades, as surely do all that is worldly. But your word lives forevermore, and that makes your work significant. You have given us worth, every breath, every action, every thought. Great things are happening, and today as we pray about those things close to our hearts, those concerns which weigh upon our souls, we seek your inspiration so that we can become your presence! Help us to get ready for your messenger, and your message. Amen.

Children's Benediction
The Lord is not slow about his promise.

Third Sunday Of Advent

Advent Wreath
We bring our fears into your revealing light.
We light this candle to acknowledge your nearness.
In the confusion of a constantly changing world
may this light guide our way into your restorative presence.

Unison Call To Worship (Psalm 126)
When the LORD restored the fortunes of Zion, we were like those who dream.
Then our mouth was filled with laughter, and our tongue with shouts of joy; then it was said among the nations, "The LORD has done great things for them."
The LORD has done great things for us, and we rejoiced.
Restore our fortunes, O LORD, like the watercourses in the Negeb.
May those who sow in tears reap with shouts of joy.
Those who go out weeping, bearing the seed for sowing, shall come home with shouts of joy, carrying their sheaves.

Unison Invocation
God of Glory, we come rejoicing, carrying our sheaves. We rejoice because you have found us, in the midst of all the distractions and headaches of the season. We confess to you this morning our earnest desire to be your people. Send your spirit in our midst, so that we might "day by day see thee more clearly, love thee more dearly, follow thee more nearly, day by day." Amen. *(from "Day By Day" by St. Richard of Chichester)*

Morning Prayer (based on Isaiah 61)
The spirit of the Lord GOD is upon us, because the LORD has anointed us; he has sent us to bring good news to the oppressed, to bind up the brokenhearted, to proclaim liberty to the captives, and release to the prisoners; to proclaim the year of the Lord's favor, and the day of vengeance of our God; to comfort all who mourn; to provide for those who mourn — to give them a garland instead of

13

ashes. We will greatly rejoice in the LORD, we shall exult in our God. For as the earth brings forth its shoots, and as a garden causes what is sown in it to spring up, so the Lord GOD will cause righteousness and praise to spring up before all the nations. Amen.

Children's Benediction
God has covered you with a robe of righteousness!

Fourth Sunday Of Advent

Advent Wreath
We hear your words, "Do not be afraid. I am with you."
Lighting this candle brings us much joy.
Your love is stronger than our fears.
May the light from this wreath surround us today and all days
with a taste of your glory.

Call To Worship

One: Do not be afraid.

All: That's easy for you to say.

Men: There's no telling what will happen when we take a risk.

Women: The world is harsh, and stuff happens.

All: We say, "Yes, the child is coming in our lives," and we can't possibly know what it means, but we'll see what happens.

One: This child is coming in our lives, this Christ child, this child of hope.

All: We take a leap in the dark, Lord, a leap of obedience. We trust you, God.

One: Let us pray.

Unison Invocation
Now as the season rushes to its conclusion, focus our hearts and minds away from the frantic distractions, our lists of to-do's, and the expectations of others, Lord, and instead lead us spiritually to Bethlehem. The Virgin Mary received an impossible word from you and she said, "Yes," perhaps without knowing fully what it might mean. We say, "Yes," to you in our worship today, not knowing fully what you have in store for us as well. Accept our wish to serve you. Fulfill your will in our lives. Amen.

Morning Prayer

Hear, O Lord, our concerns and joys, spoken and unspoken. From you nothing is hid, nor need be hidden. Hear us, Lord, and heal us. Amen.

Offering Prayer

Accept our offering this day, and use it far beyond its material worth in this world. Bless us in our giving; magnify your work in our living. Amen.

Scriptural Benediction (Romans 16:25-27)

Now to God who is able to strengthen you according to my gospel and the proclamation of Jesus Christ, according to the revelation of the mystery that was kept secret for long ages but is now disclosed, and through the prophetic writings is made known to all the Gentiles, according to the command of the eternal God, to bring about the obedience of faith — to the only wise God, through Jesus Christ, to whom be the glory forever! Amen.

Children's Benediction

I will sing of your love, forever, O Lord.

Christmas Eve/Christmas Day

Advent Wreath
What sign will you give us, Lord? The sign is not the angels. The sign is not the star. The sign is not the manger. They point to the sign. But the sign is the baby, a flesh and blood baby, someone who takes a lot of time and energy. That's our hope. We light this central candle for the King of Kings, and the Lord of Lords, a baby, the baby. Jesus. Christ.

Call To Worship (based on Isaiah 9 and Luke 2)
One: The people who walked in darkness have seen a great light; those who lived in a land of deep darkness — on them light has shined.
All: For a child has been born for us, a son given to us; authority rests upon his shoulders; and he is named Wonderful Counselor, Mighty God, Everlasting Father, Prince of Peace.
One: His authority shall grow continually, and there shall be endless peace for the throne of David and his kingdom. He will establish and uphold it with justice and with righteousness from this time onward and forevermore. The zeal of the LORD of hosts will do this.
All: Do not be afraid; for see — I am bringing you good news of great joy for all the people: to you is born this day in the city of David a Savior, who is the Messiah, the Lord.
One: This will be a sign for you: you will find a child wrapped in bands of cloth and lying in a manger.
All: Glory to God in the highest heaven, and on earth peace among those whom he favors!

Unison Invocation Prayer
Lord, the baby was the sign. The baby is still the sign. The crying baby in church, the child making noise, the middler making a mess, the teenager driving us up the wall, the young adult with goals that don't take Christ into account, the middle-ager trying to make sense

of life for having forgotten Jesus, and the senior who wonders just what happened. We're all just babies in this faith. We're not as big as we think we are. What matters is that Jesus Christ is Lord. Everything else is just details. We praise you, because Christ the Lord is born today. Amen.

Morning Prayer (based on Titus 2:11-14)
The grace of God has appeared, bringing salvation to all, training us to renounce impiety and worldly passions, and in the present age to live lives that are self-controlled, upright, and godly, while we wait for the blessed hope and the manifestation of the glory of our great God and Savior, Jesus Christ. He it is who gave himself for us that he might redeem us from all iniquity and purify for himself a people of his own who are zealous for good deeds. Amen.

Children's Benediction
For unto us a child of hope is born.

First Sunday After Christmas

Call To Worship

One: We have seen the action of the Spirit in our walk through scripture this season.

All: The Spirit overshadowed Mary and Jesus is born.

Men: Elizabeth blesses Mary, filled with the Spirit.

Women: Zechariah prophesies under the influence of the Spirit.

Right: Today we remember how Simeon was filled with the Spirit and prophesied in the temple about Jesus.

Left: Today we remember how Anna was filled with the Spirit, and how she began to praise God and to speak about the child to all who were looking for the redemption of Jerusalem.

Front: God is present among us, and the Spirit moves in our midst.

Back: We, too, will speak about the child, and about the Spirit of God.

One: As Simeon said, "This child is destined for the falling and the rising of many in Israel, and to be a sign that will be opposed ...

All: so that the inner thoughts of many will be revealed — and a sword will pierce your own soul too."

Unison Invocation

Lord of all, we know that there is no telling what might happen in our worship when your Spirit is present, but so often we want things to happen according to our schedule instead of according to your will. When Joseph and Mary brought their newborn infant to the temple they did not know Anna and Simeon would be present, nor that they would speak, but we are blessed today, thousands of years later, because they spoke. Simeon continued the song of the angels. Anna prolonged the preaching of the shepherds. The Christmas story is not over in the Bible. We pray this morning in our worship your Spirit will prolong that story in our hearts. Amen.

19

Morning Prayer

Move in our midst, Spirit of God. Call us to hear the words of our elders, our seniors who are our treasure with their wisdom. Call us to hear the cries of our children, fresh-minted from the hand of God. Call us to risk freely on their behalf as your people. Call us to celebrate our differences which make us one in you. Amen.

Morning Hymn

"Move In Our Midst" by Ken Morse (See page 113.)

Offering Prayer

Spirit of God, move in our midst. Let your generosity speak through our acts of giving and living, through the gifts of our wealth, time, energy, love, and concern for each other. Amen.

Scriptural Benediction (based on Luke 2:29-32)

Master, dismiss your servants in peace, according to your word; for our eyes have seen your salvation, which you have prepared in the presence of all peoples, a light for revelation to the Gentiles and for glory to your people Israel.

Children's Benediction

You are God's crown of beauty. Rejoice!

Second Sunday After Christmas

Unison Call To Worship (John 1:1-14)
In the beginning was the Word, and the Word was with God, and the Word was God. He was in the beginning with God. All things came into being through him, and without him not one thing came into being. What has come into being in him was life, and the life was the light of all people. The light shines in the darkness, and the darkness did not overcome it.

There was a man sent from God, whose name was John. He came as a witness to testify to the light, so that all might believe through him. He himself was not the light, but he came to testify to the light.

The true light, which enlightens everyone, was coming into the world. He was in the world, and the world came into being through him; yet the world did not know him. He came to what was his own, and his own people did not accept him. But to all who received him, who believed in his name, he gave power to become children of God, who were born, not of blood or of the will of the flesh or of the will of man, but of God.

And the Word became flesh and lived among us, and we have seen his glory, the glory as of a father's only son, full of grace and truth.

Unison Prayer
Lord, we have experienced the very human drama of Christmas, but today your word through the Evangelist John draws us into the central mystery — we praise you because in the beginning was the Word, and the Word was with God, and the Word was God. This is still so. The Word was made flesh and dwelt among us. We know you are not just a Word that speaks, but a Word that can do. You are not just thought, but action, thought put into action. How powerful is your word that is spoken and comes into being. You made worlds, you made our world, you made us. We are not frightened, but heartened. Bless us today in our gathering, fill us with the awe of your

incarnation, shelter us from that which is beyond our comprehension. Save us. Amen.

Morning Prayer
Lord Jesus, we hear the music of your word today. We hear the echo of that music in our sharing, in our prayers for each other, in the cries of our children, in the sighs of those who restlessly wait for your return. Hear our prayers. Send us clear answers. Amen.

Offering Prayer
Just as your word was made flesh and dwelt among us, we pray that our offerings, Lord, will take shape and live in your world, witnessing to the power of your word. Accept what we give in the spirit in which it is given. Amen.

Children's Benediction
And the Word was made flesh and dwelt among us.

First Sunday After The Epiphany

Call To Worship

One: Lord, your light is shining to the nations.

All: As the magi came to seek Jesus, so do we come to this light.

Men: You call us to take this light throughout the world.

Women: You call us to share this light, not hoard it.

One: Like the John the Baptist, we point to one greater than ourselves.

All: And we too, Lord, hope someday to hear you say, "You are my child, the Beloved; with you I am well pleased."

Unison Prayer

Lord, the wise still seek you, and we admit we are wise in this — that we have come to worship this morning, seeking you, praising you, testifying to you. Descend to us, this day, we pray, and fill us with your Spirit. Make us one in you, Lord, and open our hearts to all who you would send to our fellowship, that at the name of Jesus every knee should bow. These things we pray in your name. Amen.

Morning Prayer (based on Psalm 29)

The voice of the LORD flashes forth flames of fire.

The voice of the LORD shakes the wilderness; the LORD shakes the wilderness of Kadesh.

The voice of the LORD causes the oaks to whirl, and strips the forest bare; and in his temple all say, "Glory!"

The LORD sits enthroned over the flood; the LORD sits enthroned as king forever.

May the LORD give strength to his people! May the LORD bless his people with peace!

Offering Prayer

Today we call to mind the goodness of your gifts to us, your constant offering of sun and shade, stability and change, time and season. Our gifts do not match yours as our love for you cannot match your love for us. Nevertheless we come boldly forward offering you what we have, and pray that you will magnify these gifts in their work in the world. All praise and glory to you. Amen.

Children's Benediction
You are God's beloved. In you God is well pleased!

Second Sunday After The Epiphany

Call To Worship (based on Psalm 139)

All: O LORD, you have searched me and known me.

One: You know when I sit down and when I rise up; you discern my thoughts from far away.

All: You search out my path and my lying down, and are acquainted with all my ways.

One: Even before a word is on my tongue, O LORD, you know it completely.

All: You hem me in, behind and before, and lay your hand upon me.

One: Such knowledge is too wonderful for me; it is so high that I cannot attain it.

All: For it was you who formed my inward parts; you knit me together in my mother's womb.

One: I praise you, for I am fearfully and wonderfully made. Wonderful are your works; that I know very well.

All: My frame was not hidden from you, when I was being made in secret, intricately woven in the depths of the earth.

One: Your eyes beheld my unformed substance. In your book were written all the days that were formed for me, when none of them as yet existed.

All: How weighty to me are your thoughts, O God! How vast is the sum of them!

One: I try to count them — they are more than the sand; I come to the end — I am still with you.

Unison Prayer

Lord God, no one knows us like you. No one loves us like you. Yet it seems we spend the week hiding from you, concentrating on everything but you. However, this hour, this day, we resolve to focus our thoughts on you. We praise you for who you are. We praise you for what you have done. We praise you for your boundless love. Amen.

Morning Prayer

Lord of life, when Nathaniel asked if anything good could come from Nazareth, he was merely repeating the prejudice of his day. We look beyond our prejudices with your help as we see to celebrate that special glimpse we get of you in every person we meet. Bless us and guide us in our prayers for each other, so we may truly put each other's welfare first. Amen.

Offering Prayer

Lord, the earth waits expectantly for you to call everything to life. Lord, we wait expectantly for your new life to be born again in us. These gifts we bring in acknowledgment of your power which is manifested in us. As seeds planted in the snow, waiting for the spring, so we ask you call to life our gifts which with your will shall do great things. Amen.

Children's Benediction

Jesus said: Follow me!

Third Sunday After The Epiphany

Call To Worship (based on Psalm 65)

One: Praise is due to you, O God.

All: By awesome deeds you answer us with deliverance, O God of our salvation; you are the hope of all the ends of the earth and of the farthest seas.

Men: By your strength you established the mountains; you are girded with might.

Women: You silence the roaring of the seas, the roaring of their waves, the tumult of the peoples.

Right: Those who live at earth's farthest bounds are awed by your signs; you make the gateways of the morning and the evening shout for joy.

Left: You visit the earth and water it, you greatly enrich it; the river of God is full of water; you provide the people with grain, for so you have prepared it.

Front: You water its furrows abundantly, settling its ridges, softening it with showers, and blessing its growth.

Back: You crown the year with your bounty; your wagon tracks overflow with richness.

One: The pastures of the wilderness overflow, the hills gird themselves with joy,

All: the meadows clothe themselves with flocks, the valleys deck themselves with grain, they shout and sing together for joy.

Unison Prayer

God of time, the time is so urgent. You offer us joy, and we accept instead what the world has to offer. You offer us the peace that passes understanding, and we settle on the distractions of materialism. Today we have the chance to step beyond worship into discipleship. We know our history, how you have stuck by your people through thick and thin. Today we resolve, with your help, to recognize that this is the day that you have made. We will rejoice in it and be glad in it. Amen.

Morning Prayer (based on 1 Corinthians 7:29-31)
Heavenly Father, we are aware that the appointed time has grown
short. You call us to look at the creation in a different light, for the
present form of this world is passing away. We look at each other
in this new light as well. No longer, Lord, can we label people or
put them in a box. We have heard their joys this morning. We have
heard of their sufferings. We know that every person in this building is your child, that your mark is set upon them, that you desire
we all be one in you. Bless us, and hear our prayers today. Amen.

Children's Benediction
We shout and sing together for joy!

Fourth Sunday After The Epiphany

Call To Worship (based on 1 Corinthians 13)

Women: Though we speak in the tongues of mortals and of angels, but do not love, we are like a noisy gong or a clanging cymbal.

Men: And if we have prophetic powers, and understand all mysteries and knowledge ...

All: and if we have faith so as to remove mountains, but have no love, we are nothing.

Right: Love is patient. Love is kind. Love is not envious or boastful or arrogant or rude.

Left: Love does not insist on its own way; it is not irritable or resentful. It does not rejoice in wrongdoing, but rejoices in the truth.

All: Love bears all things, believes all things, hopes all things, endures all things. Love never ends.

Pastor: But as for prophecies, they will come to an end; as for tongues, they will cease; as for knowledge, it will come to an end.

All: But faith, hope, and love abide, these three, and the greatest of these is love.

Unison Invocation

Precious Lord, we are so blessed to live in an age of knowledge. We know so much more about the universe, from our own biology to our own behavior. How great you are to have created such a marvelous world. Let this knowledge be a gateway to building up your kingdom through love. Guide us as we seek to build up the body of Christ, through our time together at the table, our time together at the Bible, our time together in prayer and worship. Encourage us to seek the true knowledge that comes from Christ. Amen.

Morning Prayer
Lord, we more than acknowledge the love which called us into being — we celebrate it! Your love is the source of our being. Your love called us forth though you were sufficient unto yourself. We pray we may mirror, though through a glass darkly, that love in our fellowship here today. We hear these joys and concerns, knowing you have heard them perfectly. We wait for your answer to our petitions. In the meantime, we resolve to minister to each other. Gracious Lord, these things we pray in your holy name. Amen.

Offering Prayer
God of gifts, God of glory, these glorious gifts of yours we return to you for your work. Amen.

Children's Benediction
The fear of the Lord is the beginning of wisdom!

Fifth Sunday After The Epiphany

Call To Worship (based on Isaiah 40:28-31)
Women: Have you not known? Have you not heard? The Lord is the everlasting God, the Creator of the ends of the earth.
Men: He does not faint or grow weary; his understanding is unsearchable. He gives power to the faint and strengthens the powerless.
All: Even youths will faint and be weary, and the young will fall exhausted.
Right: But those who wait for the Lord shall renew their strength.
Left: We shall mount up with wings like eagles.
All: We shall run and not be weary. We shall walk and not be faint.

Unison Invocation
Great and powerful God, it is not always within us to run the course you have set for us as your people and as individuals. The obstacles are great and we grow weary. But with you all things are possible. Renew our strength for the tasks ahead, teach us to run together and not separately the path to salvation, arriving together to your glory. These things we pray in your great name. Amen.

Morning Prayer
We thank you for the privilege of bearing each other's burdens. We praise you for the chance to hear our sorrows and our joys. Encourage our compassion, bless our commitment, hallow our concentration upon the work of your kingdom. Amen.

Offering Prayer
For these gifts, we give you thanks, O Lord, that we have something to share for your work. We give with a glad heart, and a hopeful spirit, trusting that your wisdom will guide us as we allocate these gifts to your ministry. Amen.

Children's Benediction
We shall run and not be weary! We shall walk and not faint.

Sixth Sunday After The Epiphany

Call To Worship (based on Psalm 30)

One: I will extol you, O LORD, for you have drawn me up, and did not let my foes rejoice over me.

All: O LORD my God, I cried to you for help, and you have healed me.

Women: O LORD, you brought up my soul from Sheol, restored me to life from among those gone down to the Pit.

Men: Sing praises to the LORD, O you his faithful ones, and give thanks to his holy name.

Right: For his anger is but for a moment; his favor is for a lifetime.

Left: Weeping may linger for the night, but joy comes with the morning.

Front: Hear, O LORD, and be gracious to me! O LORD, be my helper!

Back: You have turned my mourning into dancing; you have taken off my sackcloth and clothed me with joy,

All: so that my soul may praise you and not be silent. O LORD my God, I will give thanks to you forever.

Unison Scriptural Response

Dear Lord, you tell us that weeping may linger for the night, but joy comes with the morning. Sometimes it seems like morning is a long way off. Sometimes it seems we walk in morning's light but the rest of the world huddles in darkness. Let your light shine on us, in us, and through us, so that the hope of your promises will lighten the hearts of your people everywhere. Guide our feet as we run the race of salvation. Call to us. Heal us. Save us. These things we pray in the name of your blessed and saving Son. Amen.

Morning Prayer (based on 1 Corinthians 9:24-27)

God of Challenges, we seek to run your race in such a way that all may win the prize of salvation. To do this we need self-control, and a strong will, because the prize is an imperishable one. With your help we will not run aimlessly, but proclaim to all others about your saving grace. Amen.

Offering Prayer
This day and every day we acknowledge that all we have is yours, and that what we call giving to you is simply returning but a portion of your bounty. Bless these our gifts for your work and magnify their value so they may do things greater even than our dreams. Amen.

Children's Benediction
God's favor is for a lifetime. Joy comes to us this morning.

Seventh Sunday After The Epiphany

Call To Worship (based on Isaiah 43:18-19)
Left: Remember not the former things, nor consider the things of old.
Right: Behold, I am doing a new thing; now it springs forth, do you not perceive it?
All: I will make a way in the wilderness and rivers in the desert.

Unison Invocation
Lord, we pray for your wisdom, we pray for your mercy. We pray that today you will be with us in our worship. You are creating a path where once we saw no possibilities. Bless us, mold us, re-make us, use us in your service. Sanctify us as your people this day. Amen.

Morning Prayer (based on Psalm 41)
O LORD, be gracious to me; heal me, for I have sinned against you. Be gracious to me, and raise me up. You have upheld me because of my integrity. Blessed be the LORD, the God of Israel, from everlasting to everlasting. Amen and Amen.

Offering Prayer (Psalm 41:1-2)
Happy are those who consider the poor; the LORD delivers them in the day of trouble.

The LORD protects them and keeps them alive; they are called happy in the land. You do not give them up to the will of their enemies.

Children's Benediction
Every one of God's promises is a "Yes."

Last Sunday After The Epiphany
(Transfiguration Sunday)

Call To Worship
Right: The Light has been shining.
Left: The Light of Epiphany has been shining.
Right: We have seen the coming of the kings.
Left: We have seen the coming of John the Baptist.
Right: We have seen the coming of Jesus.
Left: But the season of Epiphany is almost over.
Right: Today, with the Transfiguration, we see Jesus clearly.
Left: But in Lent the Lord is hidden in shadow.
Right: Some will follow him.
Left: Some will mock him.
Right: Some will be healed by him.
Left: Some will crucify him.
All: Let the light shine while it may. Let us all in our worship together walk to that light.

Unison Invocation
Gracious Lord, let us bask a little longer in the light of the Epiphany, the light that shines before all people. Let us savor the presence of the Lord of light. Lead us then, Lord, past the darkness of Lent, the despair of Calvary, and the sadness of the tomb, to the glory and majesty of the Resurrection. You are our hope and our salvation. You are who we most earnestly desire. Bless us as we praise you today. These things we pray in your name. Amen.

Morning Prayer
Lord, only rarely do we see each other as you see us. Only rarely are we transfigured, or transformed. For the most part our eyes are veiled from this sight. Lord, only rarely do we truly see you as you are, creator, ruler, deliverer. Open our hearts to this majestic vision. Give us the strength to bear the weight of this truth: You are glorious, and we, your creation, are reflecting this glory. Amen.

Offering Prayer

Teacher, it is good for us to be here, before your presence, offering the gifts of our wealth, our time, our talents, our energy, our commitment, our love. Accept these gifts in the spirit in which they are given and use them according to your will. Amen.

Children's Benediction

This is my Son, the Beloved; listen to him!

First Sunday In Lent

Call To Worship (based on Genesis 9:8-17 and 1 Peter 3:18-22)

One: We see your bow in the clouds, Lord of the seasons.

All: We see the signs of your faithfulness, Lord, in all seasons.

One: We know that Christ suffered for sins once for all —

All: the righteous for the unrighteous, in order to bring us to God.

One: What was true in the time of Noah, and in the time of the disciples of Jesus, is true now.

All: God's love for all is constant. We worship the God who seeks us and saves us.

Unison Prayer (based on Genesis 9:8-17 and 1 Peter 3:18-22)
Gracious Lord, when we see the rainbow in the sky, we are reminded of your covenant with all of us, believer and unbeliever, woman and man, humanity and all of creation. Your faithfulness abides in the midst of our unfaithfulness. Whether the sun is shining or is obscured by clouds, whether the rain is falling, or the waters of life are withheld, we remember with you your everlasting covenant with every living creature of all flesh that is on the earth. Thank you for your love. Abide with us in our worship today. Amen.

Offering Prayer
Lord, we feel secure in your love, and in your covenant with us as your people. Our offerings are given as a pledge of our intent to live in your word and in your promises, today and every day. Amen.

Unison Scriptural Response
Lead me in your truth, Lord. Tune my ears to the reading of your word. Set my eyes upon the rainbow. Fix my heart upon your promise. Fit my soul for repentance. Aim my life towards glory. Amen.

Children's Benediction
Lead me in your truth, and teach me, for you are the God of my salvation!

Second Sunday In Lent

Call To Worship (based on Genesis 17:1-7, 15-16)

Men: When Abram was ninety-nine years old, the LORD appeared to Abram, and said to him,

Women: "I am God Almighty; walk before me, and be blameless."

Men: We are hardly blameless.

Women: We are hardly blameless.

Men: Neither were Abram and Sarai when they became Abraham and Sarah,

Women: but you reckoned their faith unto them as righteousness.

Men: Receive our intentions, and not our actions, O Lord.

Women: Let our intentions to follow you with our hearts be reckoned as righteousness.

All: Walk before us, God Almighty. You are blameless. Teach us to be so as well.

Unison Invocation

Gracious Lord, you changed the names of Abram and Sarai and you fulfilled your promises. We worship you, all powerful God, acknowledging your goodness and pledging this day to serve you as best we may. In this Lenten season we acknowledge our sinfulness, but we celebrate your promises. Amen.

Morning Prayer (Psalm 25)

To you, O LORD, I lift up my soul.

O my God, in you I trust; do not let me be put to shame; do not let my enemies exult over me.

Do not let those who wait for you be put to shame; let them be ashamed who are wantonly treacherous.

Make me to know your ways, O LORD; teach me your paths.

Lead me in your truth, and teach me, for you are the God of my salvation; for you I wait all day long.

Be mindful of your mercy, O LORD, and of your steadfast love, for they have been from of old.

Do not remember the sins of my youth or my transgressions; according to your steadfast love remember me, for your goodness' sake, O LORD!

Good and upright is the LORD; therefore he instructs sinners in the way.

He leads the humble in what is right, and teaches the humble his way.

All the paths of the LORD are steadfast love and faithfulness, for those who keep his covenant and his decrees. Amen.

Offering Prayer

Lord, you seek to move us to new places, yet we resist, bound to one spot by our physical and spiritual possessions. Today we ask that you charge us and challenge us, in our giving, and in our life's priorities, so that when you call we may answer, without feeling fettered by the things that own us. Amen.

Children's Benediction

Teach us, O Lord, in your ways.

Third Sunday In Lent

Call To Worship (based on 2 Timothy 3:14-17)

Left: Let us continue in what you have learned and firmly believed, knowing from whom we learned it,

Right: and how from childhood we have known the sacred writings that are able to instruct us for salvation through faith in Christ Jesus.

Left: All scripture is inspired by God and is useful for teaching, for reproof, for correction, and for training in righteousness,

Right: so that everyone who belongs to God may be proficient, equipped for every good work.

Left: Open our hearts to your word in our worship.

Right: Call us to study, contemplation, adoration, and praise.

Unison Invocation

Gracious Lord, we thank you for the gift of your Word, which is a lamp unto our feet and a light unto our paths. Inspire us to seek your wisdom daily in our private and public reading of scripture that we may come to see you more clearly, love you more dearly, follow you more nearly. Amen.

Morning Prayer (Psalm 119:105-112)

Your word is a lamp to my feet and a light to my path.

I have sworn an oath and confirmed it, to observe your righteous ordinances.

I am severely afflicted; give me life, O LORD, according to your word.

Accept my offerings of praise, O LORD, and teach me your ordinances.

I hold my life in my hand continually, but I do not forget your law.

The wicked have laid a snare for me, but I do not stray from your precepts.

Your decrees are my heritage forever; they are the joy of my heart.

I incline my heart to perform your statutes forever, to the end.

Amen.

Offering Prayer
What can we offer, Lord, in response to the blessings of your word, which is a treasure in our homes and in our fellowship? We offer today, with the gifts of our wealth, our time, our energy, our love, and our concern for each other, the gift of our intent to open your book and to study its pages. Accept this offering today. Amen.

Children's Benediction
Your word is a light to my path.

Fourth Sunday In Lent

Call To Worship (based on John 3:3-17)

One: Jesus said, "Very truly, I tell you, no one can see the kingdom of God without being born from above."

All: Jesus said, "Very truly, I tell you, no one can enter the kingdom of God without being born of water and Spirit."

Women: What is born of the flesh is flesh, and what is born of the Spirit is spirit.

Men: The wind blows where it chooses, and you hear the sound of it, but you do not know where it comes from or where it goes. So it is with everyone who is born of the Spirit.

One: For God so loved the world that he gave his only Son,

All: so that everyone who believes in him may not perish but may have eternal life.

Women: Indeed, God did not send the Son into the world to condemn the world,

Men: but in order that the world might be saved through him.

Unison Invocation

God who cares, who intervenes in history through Jesus Christ, we struggle like Nicodemus to grasp the meaning of your words to us. You offer us a share in your glory. We give you only a share of our day. Bless us as your people, send your Spirit to move in our midst, that we might fully apprehend and appreciate the magnificent gift of your grace. These things we pray in the name of Jesus, who suffered and died for us, and was raised on the third day. Amen.

Morning Prayer

Lord, your children are praying. We have meditated upon our joys and our concerns, our sorrows and our celebrations. No one grieves more with us than you, no one laughs more with us than you. Turn our hearts and our minds to the suffering of your people, both within and beyond our fellowship. Let your will be fulfilled in our ministries to each other. Amen.

Offering Prayer

Lord, you offer us your Son as your salvation, and we struggle with the gift. We also struggle with our gift giving. Accept our offerings today and use them beyond their worldly measure, according to your mighty power. Amen.

Children's Benediction

God loves the world.

Fifth Sunday In Lent

Call To Worship

Women: It is not long before the journey ends.

Men: It is not long before the new life shines.

Women: It is not long before we greet the Risen Lord in Easter.

Men: It is not long before we celebrate the turning point of history.

Women: But first, Lord, create in us a new heart.

Men: But first, Lord, teach us your wisdom and truth.

Women: Give us the courage to walk with you to Calvary.

Men: Give us the strength to carry your cross for you, even if only for a short time.

All: Lord, help our weary feet to share this journey all the way through to glory.

Unison Invocation

Lord, we desire to be perfectly whole, but you, the perfect sacrifice, were broken on the cross for us. As we contemplate the broken bread of our salvation, accept our own offering of brokenness from our lives. Patch up our hearts, repair our spirits, bind our wounds, make us one body in Christ, make us whole. Precious Lord, these things we pray in your name. Amen.

Morning Prayer (based on Psalm 51:1-12)

Have mercy on me, O God, according to your steadfast love; according to your abundant mercy blot out my transgressions. Wash me thoroughly from my iniquity, and cleanse me from my sin. For I know my transgressions, and my sin is ever before me. You desire truth in the inward being; therefore teach me wisdom in my secret heart. Let me hear joy and gladness; let the bones that you have crushed rejoice. Hide your face from my sins, and blot out all my iniquities. Create in me a clean heart, O God, and put a new and right spirit within me. Do not cast me away from your presence, and do not take your Holy Spirit from me. Restore to me the joy of your salvation, and sustain in me a willing spirit. Amen.

Offering Prayer
Lord, you are our guiding star. You are the measure of all that we value. Accept our gifts as an acknowledgment at least in part of the wisdom, guidance, and forgiveness you grant us each and every day. Amen.

Children's Benediction
Restore to us the joy of salvation.

Palm Sunday

Call To Worship (based on Psalm 118:1-2, 19-29)

One: O give thanks to the LORD, for he is good; his steadfast love endures forever!

All: Let Israel say, "His steadfast love endures forever."

Women: Open to me the gates of righteousness, that I may enter through them and give thanks to the LORD.

Men: This is the gate of the LORD; the righteous shall enter through it.

Right: I thank you that you have answered me and have become my salvation.

Left: The stone that the builders rejected has become the chief cornerstone.

Front: This is the Lord's doing; it is marvelous in our eyes.

Back: This is the day that the LORD has made; let us rejoice and be glad in it.

Young: Save us, we beseech you, O LORD! O LORD, we beseech you, give us success!

Old: Blessed is the one who comes in the name of the LORD. We bless you from the house of the LORD.

All: The LORD is God, and he has given us light. Bind the festal procession with branches, up to the horns of the altar.

One: You are my God, and I will give thanks to you; you are my God, I will extol you.

All: O give thanks to the LORD, for he is good, for his steadfast love endures forever.

Unison Invocation

Humble Christ, you accepted the accolades of the crowd, but you knew too well how quickly their adulation could turn to cries of "Crucify him!" We confess that we too have praised your name, but in our actions have denied and even betrayed you. Fill us with your spirit today, so that through the waving of these palms we might not only acknowledge your Lordship, but live in such a way throughout this week that others will recognize your majesty as well. Amen.

Morning Prayer

Hosanna! Blessed is the one who comes in the name of the Lord — the King of Israel! Hosanna! Blessed is the one who comes in the name of the Lord! Blessed is the coming kingdom of our ancestor David! Hosanna in the highest heaven! Blessed is the king who comes in the name of the Lord! Peace in heaven, and glory in the highest heaven! Hosanna to the Son of David! Blessed is the one who comes in the name of the Lord! Hosanna in the highest heaven! This is the prophet Jesus from Nazareth in Galilee. Amen.

Offering Prayer

Lord Jesus, you sent your disciples to the village ahead, and told them to take charge of a colt that had never been ridden, telling them if they were challenged to say simply, "The Lord needs it and will send it back here immediately." Lord, you have every right to require an accounting from us as well, yet even when we offer our treasure you return it and request that we use it as best we can for your work. Grant us your wisdom in administering these offerings, and magnify their material worth for your work in this world. Amen.

Children's Benediction

Blessed is the one who comes in the name of the Lord!

Maundy Thursday

A First Century Communion Litany

Pastor: And regarding the thanksgiving, give thanks in this way. Regarding first the cup —

Leader: We give thanks to you, our Father, for the holy vine of your servant David, which you revealed fully in Jesus your servant.

All: Glory to you forever.

Leader: And regarding the broken bread — we give thanks to you, our Father, for the life and the knowledge which you have made known to us through your servant Jesus.

All: Glory to you forever.

Leader: For as this bread was once scattered over the mountains but was brought together into one loaf, so too gather your fellowship from the four corners of the world into your kingdom.

All: For yours are the glory and the power through Jesus Christ, forever.

(The meal follows. After the meal the Didache gives these instructions.)

Pastor: This is how you should give thanks after everyone is full.

Leader: Holy Father, we give thanks to you for your holy name, which you have planted in our hearts, and for the knowledge and faith and eternal life you have made known through Jesus your servant.

All: Glory to you forever.

Leader: All powerful ruler, who made everything with your name in mind, you gave people food and drink to make us glad so they could thank you for it. And to us you have given spiritual food and drink, and eternal life, through your servant Jesus. We thank you most of all for being all-powerful.

All: Glory to you forever.

Leader: Remember your church, Lord, and preserve it from evil, perfecting it in your love, and gathering it from the four winds, in holiness, into your kingdom which you have prepared for it.

All: For yours is the power and the glory, forever.

Leader: Let your grace come; let this world pass away.

All: Hosanna to the son of David.

Leader: If anyone is holy, let them approach. If anyone is not, let them repent. Maranatha — come soon, Lord — Amen.

(From the Didache — translated by Frank Ramirez)

Easter Sunday

Call To Worship (Psalm 118:14-24)

One: The LORD is my strength and my might; he has become my salvation.

All: There are glad songs of victory in the tents of the righteous: "The right hand of the LORD does valiantly;

One: the right hand of the LORD is exalted; the right hand of the LORD does valiantly."

All: I shall not die, but I shall live, and recount the deeds of the LORD.

One: The LORD has punished me severely, but he did not give me over to death.

All: Open to me the gates of righteousness, that I may enter through them and give thanks to the LORD.

One: This is the gate of the LORD; the righteous shall enter through it.

All: I thank you that you have answered me and have become my salvation.

One: The stone that the builders rejected has become the chief cornerstone.

All: This is the Lord's doing; it is marvelous in our eyes. This is the day that the LORD has made; let us rejoice and be glad in it.

Prayer

This is the day that the Lord has made; let us rejoice and be glad in it. For death is swallowed up in Christ's victory. We have followed the Lord through the open door and found our salvation on the other side. This is the day of our hope and our redemption. Bless us as we gather in grateful praise! Hosanna in the highest! Amen.

Unison Scriptural Response

We have seen the Lord. The Risen Lord is part of our lives now. Let us resolve to spread the glorious news that He is Risen! He is Risen Indeed!

Congregational Benediction (Isaiah 25:6-9)

One: On this mountain the LORD of hosts will make for all peoples a feast of rich food, a feast of well-aged wines, of rich food filled with marrow, of well-aged wines strained clear.

All: And he will destroy on this mountain the shroud that is cast over all peoples, the sheet that is spread over all nations; he will swallow up death forever.

One: Then the Lord GOD will wipe away the tears from all faces, and the disgrace of his people he will take away from all the earth, for the LORD has spoken.

All: It will be said on that day, Lo, this is our God; we have waited for him, so that he might save us. This is the LORD for whom we have waited; let us be glad and rejoice in his salvation.

Children's Benediction

I have seen the Lord.

Second Sunday Of Easter

Unison Confession Of Faith (1 John 1:1 — 2:2)

We declare to you what was from the beginning, what we have heard, what we have seen with our eyes, what we have looked at and touched with our hands, concerning the word of life — this life was revealed, and we have seen it and testify to it, and declare to you the eternal life that was with the Father and was revealed to us — we declare to you what we have seen and heard so that you also may have fellowship with us; and truly our fellowship is with the Father and with his Son Jesus Christ.

We are writing these things so that our joy may be complete.

This is the message we have heard from him and proclaim to you, that God is light and in him there is no darkness at all. If we say that we have fellowship with him while we are walking in darkness, we lie and do not do what is true; but if we walk in the light as he himself is in the light, we have fellowship with one another, and the blood of Jesus his Son cleanses us from all sin.

If we say that we have no sin, we deceive ourselves, and the truth is not in us. If we confess our sins, he who is faithful and just will forgive us our sins and cleanse us from all unrighteousness. If we say that we have not sinned, we make him a liar, and his word is not in us.

My little children, I am writing these things to you so that you may not sin. But if anyone does sin, we have an advocate with the Father, Jesus Christ the righteous; and he is the atoning sacrifice for our sins, and not for ours only but also for the sins of the whole world.

Morning Prayer

Lord, your disciples were of one heart. They shared all things in common. They eagerly waited for your coming. We still strive as your people to be of one heart. We want to believe that all we have we are willing to share. We eagerly wait for your coming. Accept our imperfections, and call us to greater discipleship in our devotion to you and our ministry to each other. Amen.

Offering Prayer

What can we give you, Lord, for all you have given us? Nothing, we are sure, can match your boundless gifts. Accept, then, these gifts which are tokens only of our devotion and love for you and your kingdom. Amen.

Children's Benediction

Those who believe are of one heart!

Third Sunday Of Easter

Call To Worship (based on Psalm 4)

One: Answer us when we call, O God of righteousness! Be gracious to us, and hear our prayer.

All: Know that the LORD has set apart the faithful for himself; the LORD hears when we call to him.

One: When you are disturbed, do not sin; ponder it on your beds, and be silent. Selah.

All: We offer right sacrifices, and put our trust in the LORD.

One: There are many who say, "O that we might see some good! Let the light of your face shine on us, O LORD!"

All: We will both lie down and sleep in peace; for you alone, O LORD, make us lie down in safety.

Unison Invocation

Lord, how swiftly flies this resurrection time, while we bask in your presence. The Easter season is too brief. Allow us as your people to feel, even if from afar, the rapt attention your apostles felt standing in your risen presence. Take us to a mystical place where we feel we have truly heard your word and seen your wounds. We are your people. You have promised to be with us when two or more are gathered in your name. We are gathered in your name. Surely, come Lord Jesus. Soon. Amen.

Morning Prayer

Lord, hear our joys, hear our concerns, draw us closer together as we pray with the words which your Son and our Savior taught us, saying: Our Father who art in heaven, hallowed be thy name. Thy kingdom come. Thy will be done on Earth as it is in Heaven. Give us this day our daily bread, and forgive us our debts as we forgive our debtors. And lead us not into temptation but deliver us from evil, for thine is the kingdom, the power, and the glory forever. Amen.

Offering Prayer

Now the signs of spring are all around us, the visible emblem of your resurrection. The bulbs we planted in faith last fall are flowering. You have kept faith with us once more. We keep faith with you, offering up the gifts of our wealth, our time, our treasure, our concern, our prayers, our love. Accept these offerings, we pray, and use them far beyond their material worth in the world. Amen.

Unison Benediction (Micah 4:1-4)

In days to come the mountain of the Lord's house shall be established as the highest of the mountains, and shall be raised up above the hills. Peoples shall stream to it, and many nations shall come and say: "Come, let us go up to the mountain of the LORD, to the house of the God of Jacob; that he may teach us his ways and that we may walk in his paths." For out of Zion shall go forth instruction, and the word of the LORD from Jerusalem.

He shall judge between many peoples, and shall arbitrate between strong nations far away; they shall beat their swords into plowshares, and their spears into pruning hooks; nation shall not lift up sword against nation, neither shall they learn war any more; but they shall all sit under their own vines and under their own fig trees, and no one shall make them afraid; for the mouth of the LORD of hosts has spoken.

Children's Benediction

Peace be with you.

Fourth Sunday Of Easter

Call To Worship

Women: We know love by this, that Jesus laid down his life for us.

Men: We know love as well through the parents who gave life to us.

Women: Scripture tells us that and we ought to lay down our lives for one another.

Men: And we have seen this in those parents who have lived their lives for others.

Women: The Bible says: let us love, not in word or speech, but in truth and action.

Men: The example is before us, in the lives we honor on this Mother's Day.

Women: There is no perfect parent.

Men: But there is a perfect God.

All: And this is his commandment, that we should believe in the name of his Son Jesus Christ and love one another, just as he has commanded us.

Unison Prayer

Lord, we know that all who obey your commandments abide in you, and you abide in us. We seek you first, and finding you, find your love in our brothers and sisters here in this congregation, as well as in the friends and strangers we meet in our daily lives. We seek you first, and seek to find your love in our parents. We seek you first, knowing that all things will be added unto us. Bless us in our gathering, our worshiping, and our departing today. Precious Lord, we pray things in the name of the Risen Lord. Amen.

Morning Prayer (Psalm 23 KJV)

The LORD is my shepherd; I shall not want.

He maketh me to lie down in green pastures: he leadeth me beside the still waters.

He restoreth my soul: he leadeth me in the paths of righteousness for his name's sake.

Yea, though I walk through the valley of the shadow of death, I will fear no evil: for thou art with me; thy rod and thy staff they comfort me.

Thou preparest a table before me in the presence of mine enemies: thou anointest my head with oil; my cup runneth over.

Surely goodness and mercy shall follow me all the days of my life: and I will dwell in the house of the LORD for ever.

Offering Prayer

We are your people, we are one fellowship, we are the kingdom people. With your power our meager gifts will help to make this kingdom more visible, the fellowship stronger, the people more resolute. Amen.

Children's Benediction

Little children, let us love, not in word or speech, but in truth and action.

Fifth Sunday Of Easter

Call To Worship

Right: The spirit told Philip to join the chariot of the Ethiopian.

Left: That official was puzzling over the prophet Isaiah.

Right: Philip asked, "Do you understand what you are reading?"

Left: He replied, "How can I, unless someone guides me?"

Right: And he invited Philip to get in and sit beside him.

Left: Then Philip began to speak, and starting with this scripture, he proclaimed to him the good news about Jesus.

Right: Lord, we struggle to understand your word.

Left: Guide us in our study as individuals and as a group.

Right: Send your Spirit to aid our interpretation.

Left: Let our study be with this aim in mind

All: that day by day, we may grow to see you more clearly, love you more dearly, follow you more nearly.

Unison Prayer

Dear Lord, hear our confession. You alone are Lord. You alone are worthy of praise. Guide us in our worship, guide us in our living, guide us in our giving. Accept the love we offer as we praise you for being God. Amen.

Morning Prayer

Lord, we need you every hour. How can we understand your will for our lives without you? Send your Spirit into our midst. Let our ministry to each other become a witness to your power and your love. Amen.

Offering Prayer

More than these gifts, we offer ourselves, our lives, our will, our treasure, our selves. They were always yours. Now we return them freely to you. Grant us the gift of living in accordance with your will. Amen.

Children's Benediction

I believe that Jesus Christ is the Son of God.

Sixth Sunday Of Easter

Call To Worship

Left: Is there a place where we can come to laugh?

Right: That place is here.

Men: Is there a place where we can share our sorrows?

Women: That place is here.

Right: Is there a place where we can speak to each other?

Left: That place is here.

Women: Is there a place where we can share our silence?

Men: That place is here.

All: Here in this place, where we walk with the Lord, all things are possible. Here, as we worship, God's will shall become known.

Psalm Of Praise (Psalm 98)

O sing to the LORD a new song, for he has done marvelous things. His right hand and his holy arm have gotten him victory. The LORD has made known his victory; he has revealed his vindication in the sight of the nations. He has remembered his steadfast love and faithfulness to the house of Israel. All the ends of the earth have seen the victory of our God.

Make a joyful noise to the LORD, all the earth; break forth into joyous song and sing praises. Sing praises to the LORD with the lyre, with the lyre and the sound of melody. With trumpets and the sound of the horn make a joyful noise before the King, the LORD.

Let the sea roar, and all that fills it; the world and those who live in it. Let the floods clap their hands; let the hills sing together for joy at the presence of the LORD, for he is coming to judge the earth. He will judge the world with righteousness, and the peoples with equity.

Unison Confession (1 John 5:1-6)

Everyone who believes that Jesus is the Christ has been born of God, and everyone who loves the parent loves the child. By this we know that we love the children of God, when we love God and obey his commandments. For the love of God is this, that we obey his commandments. And his commandments are not burdensome, for whatever is born of God conquers the world. And this is the victory that conquers the world, our faith.

Who is it that conquers the world but the one who believes that Jesus is the Son of God?

This is the one who came by water and blood, Jesus Christ, not with the water only but with the water and the blood. And the Spirit is the one that testifies, for the Spirit is the truth.

Children's Benediction
Love one another.

Seventh Sunday Of Easter
(Ascension Sunday)

Call To Worship (based on Acts 1:6-11)
Men: The disciples asked Jesus, "Lord, is this the time when you will restore the kingdom to Israel?"
Women: He replied, "It is not for you to know the times or periods that the Father has set by his own authority.
Left: But you will receive power when the Holy Spirit has come upon you; and you will be my witnesses in Jerusalem, in all Judea and Samaria, and to the ends of the earth."
Right: When he had said this, as they were watching, he was lifted up, and a cloud took him out of their sight.
One: While he was going and they were gazing up toward heaven, suddenly two men in white robes stood by them.
All: They said, "Men of Galilee, why do you stand looking up toward heaven? This Jesus, who has been taken up from you into heaven, will come in the same way as you saw him go into heaven."

Unison Prayer
Jesus, you reign in heaven, and we on earth recognize you as Lord. Not all the world sees this as clearly as we would like, so we pray today that you will strengthen us in spite of our weakness, so that we will not stand idly, gazing into heaven for your return, but look towards our sisters and brothers that we might serve them, and be served by them, instruct them, and learn from them as well. You are never far from us. Keep us safe, even as we walk away from the comfort of our pews into the front lines of a world that needs your gospel. Guide us. Inspire us. Save us. Amen.

Morning Prayer (based on Psalm 1)
    Lord, we are happy when we do not follow the advice of the wicked, or take the path that sinners tread. When our delight is in

your law, when we meditate on your law day and night, we become like trees planted by streams of water, yielding our fruit in its season. Our leaves do not wither. In all we do, we prosper according to your will.

God of history, we see that so often like chaff, the wind drives the wicked away. Though they seem powerful, their works come to nothing. Lord, watch over our way. Call us to be your righteous people. Amen.

Children's Benediction
You will be my witnesses.

Pentecost Sunday

Call To Worship
One: Who is like God?
All: No one is like God.
One: Who knows God fully?
All: No one knows God fully.
One: And yet who knows God?
All: God's people know God, because God has revealed God. God as Father, God as Son, God as Spirit, and God as so much more. God wants to be known. We come this morning, seeking to praise God, love God, and know God.

Unison Prayer
Lord, we know you as Father, Son, and Holy Spirit through the witness of the New Testament. We know you as one who shepherds us like lost sheep, as one who mothers us as a mother hen looks after her chicks, one who looks for us without pause, like a missing coin. We know you as engineer of the universe, the author of our stories, the farmer upon our landscape. If we cannot exhaust the depth and breadth of your person, fill us instead this morning in our worship with awe at your majesty, joy in your presence, and peace in your promises. Amen.

Morning Prayer
Like the rush of a mighty wind you are upon us. Fill our souls with the zeal of the early disciples. We pray for the Pentecost Spirit to fill us, renew us. We know we do not truly know what we pray for, or we would shrink back in holy terror at your perfect goodness, but we dare to ask. Fulfill our dream. Make us your people. Revive us again. Amen.

Morning Hymn
"Move In Our Midst" by Ken Morse (See page 113.)

Offering Prayer
Let our generosity know no bounds, Lord. In accepting our gifts, challenge us further, beyond our imaginings. Give us a glimpse of the potential of Spirit-filled humanity, and cause us to rise to the challenge. Amen.

Children's Benediction
Everyone who calls on the name of the Lord shall be saved!

Holy Trinity Sunday

Call To Worship (based on Isaiah 6:1-8)

One: In the year that King Uzziah died Isaiah saw the Lord sitting upon a throne, high and lifted up; and his train filled the temple.

All: Above the Lord stood the seraphim; each had six wings: with two he covered his face, and with two he covered his feet, and with two he flew.

One: And one called to another and said: "Holy, holy, holy is the LORD of hosts; the whole earth is full of his glory."

All: And the foundations of the thresholds shook at the voice of him who called, and the house was filled with smoke.

One: And Isaiah said: "Woe is me! For I am lost; for I am a man of unclean lips, and I dwell in the midst of a people of unclean lips; for my eyes have seen the King, the LORD of hosts!"

All: Then flew one of the seraphim to me, having in his hand a burning coal which he had taken with tongs from the altar.

One: And he touched Isaiah's mouth, and said: "Behold, this has touched your lips; your guilt is taken away, and your sin forgiven."

All: And Isaiah heard the voice of the Lord saying, "Whom shall I send, and who will go for us?" Then he said, "Here am I! Send me."

Unison Prayer Of Invocation

Lord, we thank you for the honor of calling us to the work of your kingdom. We're grateful for your presence in our midst this morning. However, this is not a great time, O Lord. There are many complications in our lives. There are a lot of distractions that are out of our control. And if we follow you there's no telling where it might lead. We know that with our baptism we said, "Here I am, send me!" But we're hoping to negotiate a better time, a little more convenient for all the things we still have to get done. Thank you again, Lord. Amen.

"A Song Of All Creation"
(11 10 11 10)
The rulers in their halls will not keep silence
Nor will the shining stars withhold their song.
As every rushing river marks the cadence
So will the seas and fountains sing along.

Our song is sung to praise the only Father.
Our song is sung to praise the only Son.
In song we praise the Holy Spirit. Gather
Our praises to all three and praise as one.

Then cry out every Angel every hour
In singing out: "Amen Amen the Lord,
The only giver of all good in power
Be praised in psalms, be praised in every word."

The rulers in their halls will not keep silence.
Nor will the shining stars withhold their song.
As every rushing river marks the cadence
So ever in the ages sing along.
(Papyrus Oxyrhynchus XV [1922] 1786, late third century, verse
translation by Frank Ramirez)

Morning Prayer (based on Romans 8:12-17, 26)
God, you have called us to be your children. We received your
Spirit, and we know this was not a spirit of slavery to fall back into
fear. When we cry, "Abba! Father!" it is the Spirit bearing witness
through us that we are children of God, and if children, then heirs,
heirs of God and fellow heirs with Christ, provided we suffer with
Christ in order that we may also be glorified with him. This is a
great matter for us, one beyond our own words, but we know like-
wise the Spirit helps us in our weakness; for we do not know how
to pray as we ought, but that very Spirit intercedes with sighs too
deep for words. You know our longing. You know our weakness.
Call us again, Lord. We answer with conviction, and we pray, with
your courage. Amen.

Offering Prayer
All we own we owe to you, God of gifts and God of glory. We offer back to you merely a portion of that which is already yours. Challenge us to greater stewardship, that we might offer you our lives as well. Amen.

Children's Benediction
Here am I! Send me.

Proper 4
Second Sunday After Pentecost

Call To Worship (based on 2 Corinthians 6:8-13)

One: The Apostle Paul wrote: "We are treated as impostors, and yet are true;

All: as unknown, and yet are well known;

Old: as dying, and see — we are alive;

Men: as punished, and yet not killed;

Women: as sorrowful, yet always rejoicing;

All: as poor, yet making many rich; as having nothing, and yet possessing everything."

One: And Paul wrote: "There is no restriction in our affections, but only in yours. In return — I speak as to children — open wide your hearts also." Let us open wide our hearts as we gather together for worship.

Unison Prayer

Lord we do not know what to make of this Christian life, rich and poor, alive and dead. But we know this — we have seen what the world calls life and it is not enough. Everything we make of our hands fails us sooner or later. But that which we build which is part of your kingdom is forever. We are so dependent upon you. We cannot cause the sun to rise, nor hold the waters in check, nor keep the stars in their courses. For us it is enough, when the storms of life are raging, that you remain our rock and our salvation. You are enough for us. We praise you. We bless you. We adore you. Stand by us when all others desert us. Amen.

Morning Prayer

What joys, what sorrows, what celebrations, what concerns, we share as your people. We thank you for the words spoken this morning. We thank you for those which are beyond words. Hear our prayers. Answer our prayers. We remain your servants. Amen.

Offering Prayer

What power, Lord, what majesty, we see in your creation. In our gardens we the result of our hard work and your faithfulness. The dreams we dreamed while gazing at seed catalogs are coming true. You have called us to hard work in our giving and in our living, and you are ever faithful. In that spirit we come today, believing that with your Spirit, all things are possible. Accept our gifts and hallow them, using them far beyond their material worth for your work in the world. Amen.

Children's Benediction

Peace! Be still!

Proper 5
Third Sunday After Pentecost

Call To Worship (based on Lamentations 3:19-26)

One: The thought of my affliction and my homelessness is wormwood and gall!

All: My soul continually thinks of it and is bowed down within me.

One: But this I call to mind, and therefore I have hope:

All: The steadfast love of the LORD never ceases, his mercies never come to an end;

One: they are new every morning; great is your faithfulness.

All: "The LORD is my portion," says my soul, "therefore I will hope in him."

One: The LORD is good to those who wait for him, to the soul that seeks him.

All: It is good that one should wait quietly for the salvation of the LORD.

Unison Invocation

Lord, your mercies never cease, your steadfast love never comes to an end. This morning we proclaim that our hope is built on nothing less than you and your faithfulness. What a blessing, what a friend we have in you. Our problems are real, our lives are complicated, our afflictions seem unceasing, but we have your promises. Today, as your people, we come to praise your name. Amen.

Unison Psalm (Psalm 130)

Out of the depths I cry to you, O LORD.

Lord, hear my voice! Let your ears be attentive to the voice of my supplications!

If you, O LORD, should mark iniquities, Lord, who could stand?

But there is forgiveness with you, so that you may be revered.

I wait for the LORD, my soul waits, and in his word I hope; my soul waits for the Lord more than those who watch for the morning, more than those who watch for the morning.

O Israel, hope in the LORD! For with the LORD there is steadfast love, and with him is great power to redeem.
It is he who will redeem Israel from all its iniquities.

Offering Litany (based on 2 Corinthians 8:7-15)

One: The Apostle Paul wrote:

All: Now as you excel in everything — in faith, in speech, in knowledge, in utmost eagerness, and in our love for you — so we want you to excel also in this generous undertaking.

Women: I do not say this as a command, but I am testing the genuineness of your love against the earnestness of others.

Men: For you know the generous act of our Lord Jesus Christ, that though he was rich, yet for your sakes he became poor, so that by his poverty you might become rich.

Young: And in this matter I am giving my advice: it is appropriate for you who began last year not only to do something but even to desire to do something —

Old: now finish doing it, so that your eagerness may be matched by completing it according to your means.

Front: For if the eagerness is there, the gift is acceptable according to what one has — not according to what one does not have.

Back: I do not mean that there should be relief for others and pressure on you, but it is a question of a fair balance between

One: your present abundance and their need, so that their abundance may be for your need, in order that there may be a fair balance.

All: As it is written, "The one who had much did not have too much, and the one who had little did not have too little."

Children's Benediction

Great is God's faithfulness!

Proper 6
Fourth Sunday After Pentecost

Call To Worship (based on Psalm 123)

All: To you I lift up my eyes, O you who are enthroned in the heavens!

One: As the eyes of servants look to the hand of their master, as the eyes of a maid to the hand of her mistress, so our eyes look to the LORD our God, until he has mercy upon us.

All: Have mercy upon us, O LORD, have mercy upon us!

Unison Invocation

Lord of glory, Lord of light, we have suffered under the weight of daily life. Our time spent here together in your presence is sweet relief. How blessed every precious moment becomes. We lift up our eyes to you, who are enthroned in the heavens, and in this haven we realize how swiftly the tyrants of our lives will pass. Your lordship is the foundation of our hope. Send your Spirit to lift our spirits! Amen.

Morning Prayer

Lord Jesus, you told us that prophets are not without honor, except in their hometown, and among their own kin, and in their own house. There are prophets in our midst. Your servants live and move and speak among us. Open our hearts that we may hear your words through their lives. Amen.

Offering Prayer

We plow the fields and scatter the good seed on the land,
but it is fed and watered by God's almighty hand.
God sends the snow in winter, the warmth to swell the grain,
the breezes and the sunshine, and soft refreshing rain.
All good gifts around us are sent from heav'n above.
We thank you Lord, we thank you, Lord, for all your love.

(Text: Matthias Claudius, *Wir pflügen und wir streuen, Fest*, 1782; tr. Jane M. Campbell, *Garland of Song*, 1861)

Children's Benediction
We look to the Lord!

Proper 7
Fifth Sunday After Pentecost

Call To Worship (based on Ephesians 1:3-14)

One: Blessed be the God and Father of our Lord Jesus Christ

All: who has blessed us in Christ with every spiritual blessing in the heavenly places.

One: In him we have redemption through his blood, the forgiveness of our trespasses,

All: according to the riches of his grace that he lavished on us.

One: With all wisdom and insight he has made known to us the mystery of his will

All: according to his good pleasure that he set forth in Christ,

One: as a plan for the fullness of time,

All: to gather up all things in him, things in heaven and things on earth.

One: In Christ we have also obtained an inheritance,

All: having been destined according to the purpose of him who accomplishes all things according to his counsel and will,

One: so that we, who were the first to set our hope on Christ, might live for the praise of his glory.

All: This is the pledge of our inheritance toward redemption as God's own people, to the praise of his glory.

Invocation

Lord, you found us; you called us. We respond to your call this morning with dedication and praise. We are gathered in your name, and while waiting for the fulfillment of history, we celebrate the glory of your plan for our lives. Bless us as your people. Together in your name we pray. Amen.

Unison Psalm (Psalm 24)

The earth is the Lord's and all that is in it, the world, and those who live in it; for he has founded it on the seas, and established it on the rivers.

Who shall ascend the hill of the LORD? And who shall stand in his holy place?

Those who have clean hands and pure hearts, who do not lift up their souls to what is false, and do not swear deceitfully.

They will receive blessing from the LORD, and vindication from the God of their salvation.

Such is the company of those who seek him, who seek the face of the God of Jacob. Selah.

Lift up your heads, O gates! and be lifted up, O ancient doors! that the King of glory may come in.

Who is the King of glory? The LORD, strong and mighty, the LORD, mighty in battle.

Lift up your heads, O gates! and be lifted up, O ancient doors! that the King of glory may come in.

Who is this King of glory? The LORD of hosts, he is the King of glory. Selah.

Offering Prayer
Day by day, Lord, we grow in appreciation of all you have done for us. Day by day our resolve grows to give in return, to the work of your church, for the glory of your name. Amen.

Children's Benediction
God is the King of glory!

Proper 8
Sixth Sunday After Pentecost

Call To Worship (based on Ephesians 2:11-22)

Women: But now in Christ Jesus we who once were far off have been brought near by the blood of Christ.

Men: For he is our peace; in his flesh he has made both groups into one and has broken down the dividing wall, that is, the hostility between us.

Left: So he came and proclaimed peace to us who were far off and peace to those of us who were near;

Right: for through him both of us have access in one Spirit to the Father.

One: So then we are no longer strangers and aliens, but we are citizens with the saints and also members of the household of God,

All: built upon the foundation of the apostles and prophets, with Christ Jesus himself as the cornerstone. In him the whole structure is joined together and grows into a holy temple in the Lord; in whom we also are built together spiritually into a dwelling place for God.

Unison Prayer

Dear Lord, we have been far from each other, not only in our travels, but in our journeys. Our goals and aims have been different, not only from each other, but from your plan for our lives. All along you have called us together, to a quiet place, where we might be nourished and filled with your spirit. Open our hearts, our minds, our souls, to your glory as we come together as one people from around our community and around our world. These things we pray in the name of the Risen Christ, Amen.

Morning Prayer

Shepherd God, you lead us, sometimes against our will, sometimes with our cooperation. Your greener pastures beckon; the waters of your stream refresh us. Your banquet awaits us. We rejoice to be part of your flock. You grieve over the loss of a single sheep. All of us, once lost, have been found. Your goodness and your mercy abide with us. We celebrate today the glorious destiny you have planned for us. As we grow to trust you with our hearts as well as our thoughts, recognizing your good will for our lives, fill us with the strong sense of your loving presence. Amen.

Offering Prayer
We recognize, O Lord, the blessings sent us from above,
Presenting for your kingdom these our offerings of love.

Children's Benediction
The Lord is my shepherd.

Proper 9
Seventh Sunday After Pentecost

Call To Worship

One: When the waves were rolling the boat about and the apostles were afraid,

All: Jesus said, "It is I. Do not be afraid."

One: Our own lives are tossed about by the storms of our everyday events.

All: Jesus says to us, "It is I. Do not be afraid."

One: When the multitudes crowded around Jesus, he asked his disciples where they might find food.

All: The task seemed impossible. Phillip said that six months' wages would not be enough to feed them all.

One: Andrew went out at least and found a boy with loaves and fishes he was willing to share.

All: Jesus commanded them to sit down and eat. Why should they have feared? It was Jesus who cared for them.

One: It is Jesus who cares for us. Let us pray.

Unison Prayer

Precious Lord, when the storms of life are raging, we seek you through the wind and rain as our guide. When the tables of the world seem bare, we count on you to give us strength so we might make a difference with your aid. When there seem to be no answers to the world's problems, we gather to praise you, knowing that there is nothing so difficult for you to answer. Bless us as your people as we praise you. Inspire us as we seek to share your word with the hungry and weary world. We pray these things in the name of the Risen Lord. Amen.

Morning Prayer (based on Ephesians 3:14-19)

We bow our knees before you, Father, from whom every family in heaven and on earth takes its name. We pray that, according to the riches of his glory, you may grant that we may be strengthened in our inner being with power through your Spirit, and that Christ may dwell in our hearts through faith, as we are being rooted and grounded in love.

We pray that we may have the power to comprehend, with all the saints, what is the breadth and length and height and depth, and to know the love of Christ that surpasses knowledge, so that we may be filled with all the fullness of God.

Unison Benediction (based on Ephesians 3:20-21)
Now to him who by the power at work within us is able to accomplish abundantly far more than all we can ask or imagine, to him be glory in the church and in Christ Jesus to all generations, forever and ever. Amen.

Children's Benediction
The Lord is near to all who call upon him.

Proper 10
Eighth Sunday After Pentecost

Call To Worship (from Psalm 78:23-29)

Right: The Lord commanded the skies above, and opened the doors of heaven;

Left: he rained down on them manna to eat, and gave them the grain of heaven.

Women: Mortals ate of the bread of angels; he sent them food in abundance.

Men: He caused the east wind to blow in the heavens, and by his power he led out the south wind;

Back: he rained flesh upon them like dust, winged birds like the sand of the seas;

Front: he let them fall within their camp, all around their dwellings.

All: And they ate and were well filled, for he gave them what they craved.

Unison Prayer

God of all gifts, even as we recall the good things you gave in the desert to your people, we remember as well their unfaithfulness, because it tells our story as well. Help us to call to mind our sins, your salvation, and the constant shower of blessings which you send to strengthen us. Bless us as we gather to worship you. Send us your holy manna. Amen.

Morning Prayer

Almighty God, we offer up one prayer for many concerns, one praise for many joys, one heart shared among this congregation for the work of God. We offer up our petitions, our wishes, our dreams, our visions, even as we pray with the words of your son and our savior, who said, "Not my will, but your will." We count upon you to sort out our conflicting prayers, our confused allegiances, and our concerns, praying boldly for what we desire even as we pray contritely for better than we deserve. Bless us as your people. These things we pray in your name. Amen.

Unison Offering Prayer
Accept, O Lord, the gifts we offer in gratitude to you for all you have done, not only for us, but for your children around the world. Amen.

Children's Benediction
God is the Father of all.

Proper 11
Ninth Sunday After Pentecost

Call To Worship

Women: God of time, the moments are yours.

Men: Weave these moments into a tapestry of your history.

Women: God of the seasons, we find satisfaction in the repetition of the familiar.

Men: We take joy in the way each season is unique.

Women: God of our gardens, we praise you for the fresh produce.

Men: We taste from afar the goodness of your garden.

All: All we have is yours, but what is yours you make ours. Your bounty is all around us. Your beauty inspires us. Your faithfulness sustains us.

Unison Prayer (based on Psalm 125)
Majestic Lord, we know that those who trust in you are like the mountains, which cannot be moved. We know you surround your people like the mountains surround Jerusalem, from this time on and forevermore. As we gather together in your name, bless us as we turn aside from our crooked ways, and do good to us as we adopt your commandments. We long to be upright in our hearts. Lead us in our worship this morning as we gather to praise your name. Amen.

Unison Offering Prayer
Accept the gifts we offer for your work and for the world. Accept our intention to serve you fully in these offerings and in our daily walk. Bless us as we work together in your name. Amen.

Morning Prayer
This day and every day, our God, we give you thanks for all your blessings unto us. Most of all, we praise your name for the gift of this fellowship we share. Call us into ministry unto each other. Fill

us with the joy that comes from sharing our daily journey. Fulfill your will in our lives together. Amen.

Children's Benediction
We trust in the Lord!

Proper 12
Tenth Sunday After Pentecost

Call To Worship (based on Proverbs 9:1-6)

One: Does not wisdom call, and does not understanding raise her voice?

All: On the heights, beside the way, at the crossroads she takes her stand;

Men: beside the gates in front of the town, at the entrance of the portals she cries out:

Women: "To you, O people, I call, and my cry is to all that live.

Front: O simple ones, learn prudence; acquire intelligence, you who lack it.

Back: Hear, for I will speak noble things, and from my lips will come what is right."

Unison Prayer

Precious Lord, we come to you this morning for wisdom and insight, praying that in our worship together your will for us can be made known. There is so much that is good in this world, but there are many distractions as well. We require your insight as we choose. Here, in this place, with your light flowing through our clear glass windows, with your natural world visible beyond our simple walls, we pray that we will feel your presence and learn your will for our lives. These things we pray in the name of the Risen Lord. Amen.

Morning Prayer

O God, ruler of all, the maker of heaven and earth and sea and all that is in them, help me, have mercy on me, wash away my sins from me, save me now and in the coming age, through our Lord and Savior Jesus Christ, through whom is the glory and the power into the age of the ages, Amen.

(Papyrus Oxyrhynchus II [1903] 407, third or fourth century, translated by Frank Ramirez)

Unison Offering Prayer
Lord of our time as well as our wealth, consecrate us as your people as we pledge to support this year's revival with our attendance, our prayers, and our hearts. Accept the gifts we lay before your altar this morning. Amen.

Children's Benediction
Let us seek God's will for our lives.

Proper 13
Eleventh Sunday After Pentecost

Call To Worship (based on Ephesians 6:10-18)

One: Be strong in the Lord and in the strength of his power.

All: Put on the whole armor of God, so that you may be able to stand against the wiles of the devil.

Men: For our struggle is not against enemies of blood and flesh, but against the rulers, against the authorities, against the cosmic powers of this present darkness, against the spiritual forces of evil in the heavenly places.

Women: Therefore take up the whole armor of God, so that you may be able to withstand on that evil day, and having done everything, to stand firm.

Right: Stand therefore, and fasten the belt of truth around your waist, and put on the breastplate of righteousness.

Left: As shoes for your feet, put on whatever will make you ready to proclaim the gospel of peace.

All: With all of these, take the shield of faith, with which you will be able to quench all the flaming arrows of the evil one.

One: Take the helmet of salvation, and the sword of the Spirit, which is the word of God.

All: Pray in the Spirit at all times in every prayer and supplication. To that end keep alert and always persevere in supplication for all the saints.

Prayer Of Praise

The rulers in their halls will not be silent
Nor will the burning stars be found lacking.
From every sea and fountain,
And every rushing river,
From every one of us
Let praises be sung.
"The Father, and the Son, and the Holy Spirit."
Let praises be sung.

Cry out, every Power, crying out:
"Amen! Amen!
Powerful Praise we give to the only giver
Of all good
Now and in the ages,
Amen! Amen!"
(Translation of P. Oxy. XV [1922] 1786, third century A.D., by Frank Ramirez)

Statement Of Commitment (based on Joshua 24:14-18)

One: Now therefore revere the LORD, and serve him in sincerity and in faithfulness.

All: Put away the gods that your ancestors served beyond the River and in Egypt, and serve the LORD.

One: Now if you are unwilling to serve the LORD, choose this day whom you will serve.

All: But as for me and my household, we will serve the LORD.

One: Then the people answered, "Far be it from us that we should forsake the LORD to serve other gods.

All: For it is the LORD our God who brought us and our ancestors up from the land of Egypt, out of the house of slavery, and who did those great signs in our sight.

One: He protected us along all the way that we went, and among all the peoples through whom we passed.

All: Therefore we also will serve the LORD, for he is our God."

Children's Benediction
We will serve the Lord.

Proper 14
Twelfth Sunday After Pentecost

Call To Worship (based on Psalm 119:105-112)
All: Your word is a lamp to my feet and a light to my path.
One: I have sworn an oath and confirmed it, to observe your righteous ordinances.
Left: I am severely afflicted; give me life, O LORD, according to your word.
Right: Accept my offerings of praise, O LORD, and teach me your ordinances.
Men: I hold my life in my hand continually, but I do not forget your law.
Women: The wicked have laid a snare for me, but I do not stray from your precepts.
Front: Your decrees are my heritage forever; they are the joy of my heart.
Back: I incline my heart to perform your statutes forever, to the end.

Unison Prayer
Your word, Lord, is our lamp and our light, as we seek to uphold your laws. We gather to praise your law, to praise your name, to praise you, God. Let your Spirit descend among us that we might become your people, perfected through your love. These things we pray in the name of the Risen Lord. Amen.

Unison Offering Prayer
Our offerings we bring today, and pray you will receive them in the spirit that they are given for the work of your church throughout the world. Amen.

Morning Prayer
Lord, we seek to be doers of the word, and not merely hearers. It's so easy for us to lose sight of what we have pledged to do in your

name. Grant that in our hearing of the joys and concerns, the sorrows and the celebrations, of our fellow Christians, our sisters and brothers in the Lord, we may be inspired to comfort, cajole, and constantly abide with each other, praying for each other, and with each other, remembering the words of your Son and our Savior, saying in one voice:

Our Father, who art in heaven, hallowed be thy name. Thy kingdom come. Thy will be done on Earth as it is in Heaven. Give us this day our daily bread. Forgive us our debts as we forgive our debtors. And lead us not into temptation, but deliver us from evil, for thine is the kingdom, the power, and the glory, forever. Amen.

Children's Benediction
Your word is a light unto our path.

Proper 15
Thirteenth Sunday After Pentecost

Call To Worship (based on Psalm 146)

All: Praise the LORD! Praise the LORD, O my soul!

One: I will praise the LORD as long as I live; I will sing praises to my God all my life long.

Women: Do not put your trust in princes, in mortals, in whom there is no help.

Men: When their breath departs, they return to the earth; on that very day their plans perish.

Right: Happy are those whose help is the God of Jacob, whose hope is in the LORD their God,

Left: who made heaven and earth, the sea, and all that is in them; who keeps faith forever;

Front: who executes justice for the oppressed; who gives food to the hungry. The LORD sets the prisoners free;

Back: the LORD opens the eyes of the blind. The LORD lifts up those who are bowed down; the LORD loves the righteous.

One: The LORD watches over the strangers; he upholds the orphan and the widow, but the way of the wicked he brings to ruin.

All: The LORD will reign forever, your God, O Zion, for all generations. Praise the LORD!

Unison Prayer

Lord of hosts, in a changing world you are the one constant. There is no shadow of turning with you. Let your Spirit descend in our midst as we gather to worship you, praise you, and dedicate our lives to you. Bless us as we seek to minister to each other and to the wide world beyond our doors. These things we pray in the name of the Risen Jesus. Amen.

Statement Of Mutual Encouragement (based on Isaiah 35:4-9)
We say to those who are of a fearful heart, "Be strong, do not fear! Here is your God. He will come and save you." Then the eyes of the blind shall be opened, and the ears of the deaf unstopped; then the lame shall leap like a deer, and the tongue of the speechless sing for joy. For waters shall break forth in the wilderness, and streams in the desert; the burning sand shall become a pool, and the thirsty ground, springs of water; the haunt of jackals shall become a swamp, the grass shall become reeds and rushes.

A highway shall be there, and it shall be called the Holy Way; the unclean shall not travel on it, but it shall be for God's people; no traveler shall go astray. No lion shall be there, nor shall any ravenous beast come up on it; they shall not be found there, but the redeemed shall walk there.

Children's Benediction
Be strong. Do not fear!

Proper 16
Fourteenth Sunday After Pentecost

Call To Worship (based on Proverbs 1:20-33 and Mark 8:27-29)

One: Wisdom cries out in the street; in the squares she raises her voice.

All: At the busiest corner she cries out; at the entrance of the city gates she speaks:

Women: How long, O simple ones, will you love being simple? How long will scoffers delight in their scoffing and fools hate knowledge?

Men: Give heed to my reproof; I will pour out my thoughts to you; I will make my words known to you.

Right: Jesus asked, "Who do people say that I am?"

Left: Peter said, and we say, "You are the Messiah."

One: For waywardness kills the simple, and the complacency of fools destroys them;

All: but those who listen to me will be secure and will live at ease, without dread of disaster.

Unison Invocation

Lord Jesus, you asked your disciples, "Who do people say that I am?" They were unwilling to be wrong, so they hedged. But you asked Peter, and even though his understanding was not complete, even though he was unsure about your role as a suffering servant, he answered, "You are the Messiah."

Lord Jesus, you are the Messiah. You are Savior. You are king. Whatever we may have yet to learn as your disciples, these simple statements we make today and every day. Amen.

Morning Prayer (based on Mark 8:34-38)

Lord Jesus, you said, "If any want to become my followers, let them deny themselves and take up their cross and follow me. For those who want to save their life will lose it, and those who lose their life for my sake, and for the sake of the gospel, will save it."

What will it profit us, Lord, to gain the whole world, and forfeit our life? What can the world offer in return? We are not ashamed of you. We praise you and proclaim you this morning. When you come in glory we pray that you will recognize us as your people. We serve each other. We proclaim your name. We minister to your kingdom. We love you, Lord Jesus. Amen.

Children's Benediction
Jesus is the Messiah.

Proper 17
Fifteenth Sunday After Pentecost

Call To Worship

All: Lord, we come together, restless in our pews.

One: Our gaze drifts outside to the corn, ripe for harvest, and to the cars that pass.

Men: We wonder what errands they have.

Women: We ponder our own errands later this day.

All: Lord, we come together, restless in our lives.

One: Our thoughts drift to the days of our lives, so many and so few.

Left: We think about where we are going, what our lives hold.

Right: We think about what we have done, the chapters of our own story.

Front: We ponder our successes.

Back: We ponder our failures.

All: Lord, we offer all of this to you, our restlessless, our regrets, our hopes, and our devotion. Mold us, your imperfect clay, into your perfect church.

Unison Prayer

Gracious Lord, this day we resolve again to be your presence in a difficult world. Fill us with your spirit, repair the cracks in our broken lives, perfect us in your image, lead us to your glory. Bless us in our gathering together and in our leaving here today. Amen.

Morning Prayer

Lord, so often we value people by what they can do for us, yet you weigh us in a different scale. In your kingdom the broken, the marginalized, the abandoned, the worthless, the foreigner, the outcast, the prisoner, the diseased, the contagious, the imprisoned, the noisy, the annoying, these are the ones you use, these are your tools for the work of your kingdom. We want to see with your eyes, hear with your ears, love with your heart. Amen.

Unison Offering Prayer
Lord, our offerings are given from that which we value most, our wealth, for those things we understand least, the actions of your Spirit in this world. Magnify our offerings, magnify your Spirit in our hearts. Amen.

Children's Benediction
Jesus said, "Whoever welcomes a child welcomes me."

Proper 18
Sixteenth Sunday After Pentecost

Call To Worship

All: The harvest is before us. But someone has to gather the crops.

One: God's good earth once again provides us with bounty to feed ourselves and others.

Women: We gather together to ask the Lord's blessings ...

Men: not only for ourselves but for all.

Left: We Christians call ourselves by many names.

Right: But today as we break the bread and share the cup in your name ...

All: we are one people.

Unison Prayer

Lord and God, we thank you for the unity which binds us all together as disciples. We praise your name for women and men throughout the world who believe in your goodness and share together this remembrance. Bless us in our actions today and throughout the week. These things we pray in the name of the Risen Jesus. Amen.

Prayer Of Thanksgiving For World Communion Sunday

Blessed be the Lord Christ, the King of the Universe who created all things, apportioned food, appointed drink to all the children of flesh in which they will be satisfied, but gave to us who are in the form of humans to eat from the same food as the numerous swarms of angels, and because of all this we are led to bless God in the raising of voices in the tumult of the people.

(Dura-Europos Parchment D, 25, second half of third century, a Hebrew Christian prayer of Thanksgiving, translated by Frank Ramirez)

Children's Benediction

Be at peace with one another.

Proper 19
Seventeenth Sunday After Pentecost

Call To Worship (based on Psalm 8)

One: O LORD, our Sovereign, how majestic is your name in all the earth! You have set your glory above the heavens.

All: Out of the mouths of babes and infants you have founded a bulwark because of your foes, to silence the enemy and the avenger.

Women: When I look at your heavens, the work of your fingers, the moon and the stars that you have established;

Men: what are human beings that you are mindful of them, mortals that you care for them?

Left: Yet you have made them a little lower than God, and crowned them with glory and honor.

Right: You have given them dominion over the works of your hands; you have put all things under their feet,

Front: all sheep and oxen, and also the beasts of the field,

Back: the birds of the air, and the fish of the sea, whatever passes along the paths of the seas.

All: O LORD, our Sovereign, how majestic is your name in all the earth!

Unison Prayer

Lord of all we see and cannot see, creation praises you through all the seasons. We praise you because we are in such awe of what you have made. The more we learn about the world and the universe, the more impressed we become. How great you are, O Lord, how majestic is your name in all the earth! We praise you, and pray that we will be able to tell others about what you have done for us. Amen.

Morning Prayer

Lord of our lives, we offer you our lives, our joys and our sorrows, our concerns and our cares. Hear us in our suffering, share with us our happiness. We ask you to be especially present with those who have lost loved ones, with those who may face trials, with those who need healing. We pray for those who cannot be with us today. Draw us closer as your family, both here in this building and with others of good will around the world. Let the experiences of our lives point our hearts and minds towards you. Amen.

Unison Offering Prayer
We give you, Lord, only a portion of what you have given us. We give this freely and with a cheerful heart. Bless us, Lord in our giving, and use these gifts magnificently for the work of the kingdom throughout the world. Amen.

Children's Benediction
O Lord, how majestic is your name in all the earth!

Proper 20
Eighteenth Sunday After Pentecost

Call To Worship

One: Lord, we call to mind the hatred and violence half a world away

All: and we pray for your peace that passes understanding to descend on our world.

Men: Lord, we think of the unrest in our own hearts and souls

Women: and we pray for the rest you have promised in your word.

Right: Lord, we think of those who suffer daily from physical and emotional pain

Left: and we pray that your healing will engulf those who need it most.

Front: Do not forget us, Lord. Be with us today in our worship.

Back: Stay with us, Lord, beyond our worship into our living.

All: Inspire us today to work for peace and healing.

Unison Prayer

Gracious Lord, you are the source of our hope. We read the headlines and wonder what is in the hearts of those who prefer hatred. Heal that hatred, and help us look into our own hearts for the ways in which we have nurtured grudges, hatred, fear, and prejudice. Even as the crops are taken out of the field in a great harvest, help us to reap a greater harvest that comes from the seeds of your charity that have been planted by you in our hearts. You are the source of hope, the source of peace, the source of healing. Let us become your will upon this earth. Let there be peace upon this earth. Amen.

Morning Prayer (based on Amos 5:6-15)

Lord, we seek good and not evil. Be with us as you have said. You who made the Pleiades and Orion, who turns deep darkness into the morning, and darkens the day into night, who calls for the waters of the sea, and pours them out on the surface of the earth, you whose name is Lord, we seek you that we might live. With your help we shall hate evil and love good, and establish justice in the public places. This is our challenge. This is your will for our lives. Bless us as your people in this endeavor. Amen.

Unison Offering Prayer
Accept our offerings, Lord, in the spirit in which they are given. Magnify our offerings in their work for your word. Amen.

Children's Benediction
Seek good and not evil that you may live.

Proper 21
Nineteenth Sunday After Pentecost

Call To Worship (based on Mark 10:35-45)

All: The disciples had a request for Jesus. They said: "Grant us to sit, one at your right hand and one at your left, in your glory."

One: But Jesus said to them, "You do not know what you are asking. Are you able to drink the cup that I drink, or be baptized with the baptism that I am baptized with?"

All: They replied, "We are able."

One: Then Jesus said to them, "The cup that I drink you will drink; and with the baptism with which I am baptized, you will be baptized;

All: but to sit at my right hand or at my left is not mine to grant, but it is for those for whom it has been prepared."

One: Jesus told us:

All: "Whoever wishes to become great among you must be your servant, and whoever wishes to be first among you must be slave of all. For the Son of Man came not to be served but to serve, and to give his life a ransom for many."

One: Lord —

All: we are able.

Unison Invocation

Lord, we are able, or at least we earnestly wish to proclaim so. We cannot possibly know what lies ahead — what trials we may endure in your name, or what it may cost us to be proclaimed your disciples. We count upon you to strengthen our resolve when things get tough, and to be the light for our path when all becomes dark. Hear us now, while we are strong, and shelter us, when we are weak. We are able, though you will justify us. Amen.

Unison Psalm (Psalm 91)

You who live in the shelter of the Most High, who abide in the shadow of the Almighty, will say to the LORD, "My refuge and my fortress; my God, in whom I trust."

For he will deliver you from the snare of the fowler and from the deadly pestilence; he will cover you with his pinions, and under his wings you will find refuge; his faithfulness is a shield and buckler.

You will not fear the terror of the night, or the arrow that flies by day, or the pestilence that stalks in darkness, or the destruction that wastes at noonday.

A thousand may fall at your side, ten thousand at your right hand, but it will not come near you. You will only look with your eyes and see the punishment of the wicked.

Because you have made the LORD your refuge, the Most High your dwelling place, no evil shall befall you, no scourge come near your tent.

For he will command his angels concerning you to guard you in all your ways. On their hands they will bear you up, so that you will not dash your foot against a stone. You will tread on the lion and the adder, the young lion and the serpent you will trample under foot.

Those who love me, I will deliver; I will protect those who know my name. When they call to me, I will answer them; I will be with them in trouble, I will rescue them and honor them. With long life I will satisfy them, and show them my salvation.

Offering Prayer

We offer up to you that which is yours, and especially today we offer up our desire to be servants to each other, and to your people near and far. Amen.

Children's Benediction

Lord, we are able!

Proper 22
Twentieth Sunday After Pentecost

Call To Worship (based on Psalm 34:1-8)

One: I will bless the LORD at all times; his praise shall continually be in my mouth.

All: My soul makes its boast in the LORD; let the humble hear and be glad.

One: O magnify the LORD with me, and let us exalt his name together.

All: I sought the LORD, and he answered me, and delivered me from all my fears.

One: Look to him, and be radiant; so your faces shall never be ashamed.

All: This poor soul cried, and was heard by the LORD, and was saved from every trouble.

One: The angel of the LORD encamps around those who fear him, and delivers them.

All: O taste and see that the LORD is good; happy are those who take refuge in him.

Unison Prayer

Lord, if we are radiant, it is because the light of your love is shining off our faces this morning. We are your people, and you have remembered to call us together. What a blessing at all times it is that we can gather together in your name and become your people. What a greater blessing that a feast in your honor is planned today. We will not forget the sacrifice of Jesus, and will continue to follow his example in bending our knees and washing the feet of our sisters and brothers, breaking the bread of the Love Feast, and sharing the cup of the new covenant, which brings life to all. In our time together we see you. Be present with us today in our worship and in our Love Feast. Amen.

Morning Prayer

What a privilege, Lord Jesus, to abide among your people today! What a joy it is to stand and sit and kneel with sisters and brothers in Christ. We are close to you when we are close to each other, and closer still when we pray with the words you taught us, saying in one voice:

Our Father, who art in heaven, hallowed be thy name. Thy kingdom come. Thy will be done on Earth as it is in Heaven. Give us this day our daily bread, and forgive us our debts as we forgive our debtors. And lead us not into temptation, but deliver us from evil, for thine is the kingdom, the power, and the glory, forever. Amen.

Offering Prayer

Lord, this day and this day only we have the chance to answer this day's call. Bless us as your people in our giving and in our living. Amen.

Children's Benediction

God is calling you.

Proper 23
Twenty-first Sunday After Pentecost

Call To Worship (Psalm 146)

One: Praise the LORD! Praise the LORD, O my soul!

All: I will praise the LORD as long as I live; I will sing praises to my God all my life long.

Women: Do not put your trust in princes, in mortals, in whom there is no help.

Men: When their breath departs, they return to the earth; on that very day their plans perish.

Front: Happy are those whose help is the God of Jacob, whose hope is in the LORD their God,

Back: who made heaven and earth, the sea, and all that is in them; who keeps faith forever;

One: who executes justice for the oppressed; who gives food to the hungry. The LORD sets the prisoners free;

All: the LORD opens the eyes of the blind. The LORD lifts up those who are bowed down; the LORD loves the righteous.

Women: The LORD watches over the strangers; he upholds the orphan and the widow, but the way of the wicked he brings to ruin.

Men: The LORD will reign forever, your God, O Zion, for all generations. Praise the LORD!

Unison Prayer

Lord of the Harvest, Lord of Life, we praise you and beg you to descend and live among us today. You are our hope in this troubled world. You are the peace that passes understanding. Guide us today in our worship. Inspire us and lead us with this good news, this gospel, into those troubled areas which need it most. Bless us in our gathering. Lord, these things we pray, trusting in your everlasting reign. Amen.

Offering Prayer

Day by day, Lord, we pray that we shall dedicate our lives, our substance, and our intentions to your work in the world. Amen.

Children's Benediction

Praise the Lord, O my soul!

Proper 24
Twenty-second Sunday After Pentecost

Unison Call To Worship (Psalm 127:1-2)
Unless the LORD builds the house, those who build it labor in vain. Unless the LORD guards the city, the guard keeps watch in vain.

It is in vain that you rise up early and go late to rest, eating the bread of anxious toil; for he gives sleep to his beloved.

Unison Prayer Of Invocation
Lord, let us not build in vain. You are the foundation of our faith. Keep guard upon our thoughts. You are the source of our rest. Though we work anxiously for the things of the world, let us never lose sight, with your vision O Lord, of the things that truly last. Our worship this morning in part at least will remind us of your kingdom and our obligations to praise you, and to raise our hands in love and adoration. Amen.

Morning Prayer
There are no ordinary people among us, Lord, and for that we give you thanks. Each person here, each person who longs to be here but is prevented, each person who may be here with us in the future, bears your mark, reveals your likeness, tells us something about you that only they can say. Challenge us to treasure this marvelous gift which you have sent among us. Bless us through our time of sharing and caring. Amen.

Offering Reading (Mark 12:38-44)
As (Jesus) taught, he said, "Beware of the scribes, who like to walk around in long robes, and to be greeted with respect in the marketplaces, and to have the best seats in the synagogues and places of honor at banquets! They devour widows' houses and for the sake of appearance say long prayers. They will receive the greater condemnation."

He sat down opposite the treasury, and watched the crowd putting money into the treasury. Many rich people put in large sums. A poor widow came and put in two small copper coins, which are worth a penny. Then he called his disciples and said to them, "Truly I tell you, this poor widow has put in more than all those who are contributing to the treasury. For all of them have contributed out of their abundance; but she out of her poverty has put in everything she had, all she had to live on."

Children's Benediction
Let us give all we have!

Proper 25
Twenty-third Sunday After Pentecost

Call To Worship (based on Psalm 16)

One: Protect me, O God, for in you I take refuge.

All: I say to the LORD, "You are my Lord; I have no good apart from you."

Women: The LORD is my chosen portion and my cup; you hold my lot.

Men: The boundary lines have fallen for me in pleasant places; I have a goodly heritage.

Front: I bless the LORD who gives me counsel; in the night also my heart instructs me.

Back: I keep the LORD always before me; because he is at my right hand, I shall not be moved.

Young: Therefore my heart is glad, and my soul rejoices; my body also rests secure.

Old: For you do not give me up to Sheol, or let your faithful one see the Pit.

All: You show me the path of life. In your presence there is fullness of joy; in your right hand are pleasures forevermore.

Unison Invocation
Lord of time, we praise you for the precious moments we have today to praise your name and seek your will for our lives. For most of us the boundary lines have fallen in pleasant places. We are luckier and more privileged than most people the world over, and better off than many in our communities. Call us to service and sacrifice, and bless us in our time together today. Amen.

Morning Prayer (based on Daniel 12:1-3)
Lord, how we wait for our protector. How we wait for our deliverance. You have said that many of those who sleep in the dust of the earth shall awake, some to everlasting life, and some to shame and

everlasting contempt. We know that those who are wise shall shine like the brightness of the sky, and those who lead many to righteousness, like the stars forever and ever. Satisfy our longing, Lord, for your justice. Satisfy our yearning for your salvation. Satisfy our hope for your reward. Amen.

Offering Prayer
Lord, we thank you for the work of our church board members. We thank you for all the gifts given today. Amen.

Children's Benediction
You show me the path of life!

Proper 26
Last Sunday After Pentecost

Call To Worship (based on Revelation 1:8)
"I am the Alpha and the Omega," says the Lord God, who is and
who was and who is to come, the Almighty.

Let all mortal flesh keep silence, and with fear and trembling stand.
Ponder nothing earthly minded, for with blessing in his hand
Christ our God to earth descendeth, our full homage to demand.

Rank on rank the host of heaven spreads its vanguard on the way,
as the Light of light descendeth from the realms of endless day,
that the pow'rs of hell may vanish as the darkness clears away.

At his feet the six-winged seraph, cherubim with sleepless eye,
veil their faces to the Presence, as with ceaseless voice they cry,
"Alleluia! Alleluia! Alleluia, Lord Most High!"
(*Liturgy of St. James of Jerusalem*, fifth c.; translated by Gerard
Moultrie, *Lyra Eucharistica,* second edition, 1864)

Unison Prayer
Now we praise you, now we raise our voices, now the ways of
your mercy are revealed to us. Christ the King we gladly sing of,
now you bring love to us here. What we guess as through a glass
that is dark will soon bless in revealed glory as the story which we
tell to the nations is proven true. Amen.

Morning Prayer
Lord, hear our many prayers today. We sorrow with those who are
suffering, and rejoice with those who are glad. We lift up those
who face trials and ask your blessings for those who have endured
difficult times. Bless us as your family in all our experiences. Amen.

Offering Prayer
God of time, the liturgical year is ending, even though our worldly calendar does not keep pace. Eternity is measured by a different clock, and none of us knows when the hour will strike and your glory will appear. In our offerings today we seek, by supporting your work, to make that veiled glory visible, if only a pale reflection, that others may seek you as we seek you. Hallow our offerings and make them an instrument of your peace. Amen.

Children's Benediction
Look! He is coming with the clouds!

Move in our midst

PINE GLEN 99. 99

1 Move in our midst, thou Spir - it of God.
2 Touch thou our hands to lead us a - right.
3 Strike from our feet the fet - ters that bind.
4 Kin - dle our hearts to burn with thy flame.

Go with us down from thy ho - ly hill.
Guide us for - ev - er, show us thy way.
Lift from our lives the weight of our wrong.
Raise up thy ban - ners high in this hour.

Walk with us through the storm and the calm.
Trans - form our dark - ness in - to thy light.
Teach us to love with heart, soul, and mind.
Stir us to build new worlds in thy name.

Spir - it of God, go thou with us still.
Spir - it of God, lead thou us to - day.
Spir - it of God, thy love makes us strong.
Spir - it of God, O send us thy pow'r!

Text: Kenneth I. Morse, 1942, 1949, *The Brethren Hymnal*, 1951
Music: Perry I. Huffaker, 1950, *The Brethren Hymnal*, 1051
Text and Music copyright © 1950 Church of the Brethren General Board.

113